Goodnight Prayers

Illustrated by Jill Barklem

LITTLE LIONS

Sunday

Father, unto you we raise
Hearts and voices full of praise.
Bless us waking, guard us sleeping,
Through this night and all our days.

Glory to thee, my God, this night
For all the blessings of the light;
Keep me, O keep me, King of kings,
Beneath thy own almighty wings.

Tuesday

Jesus, tender Shepherd, hear me;
Bless your little lamb tonight;
Through the darkness
    please be near me;
Keep me safe till morning light.

All this day your hand has led me,
And I thank you for your care;
You have warmed and clothed
    and fed me;
Listen to my evening prayer.

Wednesday

O God, our heavenly Father,
bless and keep your children
all over the world,
this night and for ever.

Thursday

Jesus, friend of little children,
Be a friend to me;
Take my hand and ever keep me
Close to thee.

Friday

Loving Father, I'm sorry
for the wrong things that I have
said or thought or done today.
I'm sorry if I made others unhappy,
but most of all, help me
to be sorry if I have hurt you.

God the Father, bless us;
God the Son, defend us;
God the Spirit, keep us
Now and evermore.

Saturday

In our work and play God leads us,
Every step we take.
In our sleep he will be near us,
Watching till we wake.

Copyright © 1975 Lion Publishing
Published by
Lion Publishing plc
Icknield Way, Tring, Herts, England
ISBN 0 85648 032 0
Lion Publishing Corporation
772 Airport Boulevard, Ann Arbor, Michigan 48106, USA
ISBN 0 85648 032 0
Albatross Books
PO Box 320, Sutherland, NSW 2232, Australia
ISBN 0 86760 300 3
First edition 1975
Reprinted 1981, 1983
Printed by Artes Gráficas Toledo, S.A. Spain

D. L. TO: 689-1983

Acknowledgements
'Jesus, friend of little children' by W. J. Mathams from *Songs of Praise*,
Oxford University Press. 'Loving Father, I'm sorry' by Zinnia Bryan from
Let's Talk to God, Scripture Union.